What they don't

CHARLES I
AND THE
CIVIL WAR

By Bob Fowke
(with drawings by the same)

Dedicated to *Arise Evans*, prophet.
He made people laugh ...

Hodder
Children's

e Limited

Text and illustrations, copyright © Bob Fowke 2001

The right of Bob Fowke to be identified as the author of the work has been asserted by him in accordance with the Copyright, Designs and Patents Act 1988.

Produced by Fowke & Co. for Hodder Children's Books

Cover photo: Portrait of King Charles I (1600-49) by Sir Anthony van Dyck (1599-1641). Workshop of Philip Mould, Historical Portraits Ltd, London, UK/Bridgeman Art Library.

Published by Hodder Children's Books 2001

0340 788062

10 9 8 7 6 5 4 3 2 1

Hodder Children's Books
a Division of Hodder Headline Limited
338 Euston Road
London NW1 3BH

Printed and bound by the Guernsey Press Co. Ltd., Channel Islands
A Catalogue record for this book is available from the British Library

CONTENTS

OFF WITH HIS HEAD!

COUNTRY LIFE AND
COUNTRY STRIFE

LAST OF THE LITTER

PROBLEMS WITH PARLIAMENT

WAR!

BESIEGED!

GODLY MEN - AND MAD MEN

WIVES AND WITCHES

Watch out for the *Sign of the Foot*! Whenever you see this sign
in the book it means there are some more details at the *FOOT* of
the page. Like here.

OFF WITH HIS HEAD!

TO BEGIN AT THE END

One cold afternoon on 30 January 1649, a short, anxious-looking king was executed outside the Palace of Whitehall in London. His head came off with a single blow of the axe. As it did so, a sort of low groan went up from the watching crowd.

Thus ended the trial and execution of King Charles I, the only official execution of a king in British history. It was the climax of the English Civil War. The events which led up to it were some of the maddest, and yet the saddest, in British history.

SPLIT HAIRS

The English Civil War (1642-51) was fought between the supporters of the king Charles I on one side and the supporters of Parliament on the other side. Parliament won and Charles lost - his head.

The war split the country down the middle. Fathers found themselves fighting on opposite sides to their sons, and brothers on opposite sides to brothers. As the Royalist general Hopton wrote to the Roundhead general Waller before a battle:

> *With what perfect hatred I detest this war without an enemy ...*

The supporters of Parliament, or *Parliamentarians*, were commonly called *Roundheads*, because at the start of the war a lot of them wore their hair cut short, 'in little peakes as was something ridiculous to behold'. The supporters of the King were known as *Royalists* or *Cavaliers*, from the French word *chevalier* meaning a knight. The Cavalier fashion was for long flowing locks with ribbons.

Actually both sides wore their hair fairly long by modern standards for most of the war and they didn't look very different from each other.

THE KING THING

In the seventeenth century, all the big European countries were ruled by kings. The theory was that God had put them on their thrones - so they didn't need to be elected . The king was the Deputy Headmaster, so to speak, and God was the Headmaster. This theory was known as the 'Divine Right of Kings'. Charles I was (naturally) very keen on it.

Actually, some kings *have been* elected, after a fashion. The Saxon kings were chosen by their leading noblemen and any important member of the royal family could be chosen.

Well, Charles may have *believed* in the Divine Right of Kings, but it didn't do him any good. Other European kings had large numbers of lords and ladies to help them rule and large armies to back them up, but England was different. Charles and other English kings had no army worth speaking of and there were very few English lords and ladies.

THE GENTRY THING

In England there were just 122 lords and a mere two thousand knights compared to *tens of thousands* of such nobles in countries such as France and Germany. This meant that the English king had to rely on the ordinary 'gentry'  to help run things. The gentry were country squires and such like, the sort of people who lived in the big 'hall' in most villages. Because there were so few lords, the king simply couldn't afford to upset the gentry if he wanted the country to run smoothly.

 Gentry is a group word for 'gentlemen'.

THE MAN WHO NOSE

In this picture, the higher the class of a person,
the longer their nose. There are four classes:
king, nobles, gentry and common people.
How many are there of each class?
(Answer on page 122.)

The Parliament thing

Parliament, in particular the House of Commons, was the talking shop of the gentry . It was where their representatives met to discuss problems. It was through Parliament that the gentry could let the king know if they were upset about anything. In return they voted to raise taxes so that he had enough money to run the country - at least that was the theory.

Parliament wasn't very keen on the Divine Right of Kings, not if the king did things that annoyed them. Fat lot Charles cared: he behaved like God's Deputy Headmaster, whether they liked it or not - he had all the management skills of a bad-tempered ostrich.

Members of the House of Commons were elected by the property-owning part of the population. There was no 'votes for all' in those days.

The War thing

Charles quarrelled with Parliament quite early on in his reign (1625-49). He tried to rule without it, failed - and ended up going to war with it! Hardly good management by any standards.

The war lasted from 1642-51 . Incidentally, and just to cheer things up, it was fought during a period when the British weather was at its lousiest. Most of the events described in this book took place in rain, cold or fog, and often in all three.

Put on your wellies and let's get started ...

The Civil war is usually divided into parts: the *First Civil War*, 1642-46, the *Second Civil War*, 1648-9, and the *Third Civil War*, 1650-51.

COUNTRY LIFE AND COUNTRY STRIFE

VILLAGE MATTERS
PEOPLE FACTS

People were spread thinly in seventeenth century Britain. The total population of the British Isles was around seven million, compared to sixty million today. Even London, by far the largest town, had a population of only 250,000. The next biggest cities, such as York and Norwich, were the size of small market towns.

Most people lived in the countryside where they were either farmers or farm labourers. In those days, as far as the majority was concerned, you grew your own food or you went hungry.

OUR LAST CABBAGE!

The population stayed small, or grew slowly, for two main reasons:

1. A lot of babies and young children died young. This was hardly surprising considering how dirty everybody was, what poor food some of them ate and how little they knew about medicine.

2. People got married late. The average age of marriage for women was around twenty-six and for men it was around twenty-eight. They waited to marry until they could have a house or cottage of their own. This might mean waiting until their parents died or until the man had finished a long apprenticeship  . Since women can only have babies between the ages of about fifteen to forty-five, late marriage meant that a lot of the time when they could have been having babies, they weren't.

An *apprentice* is someone who is learning a trade. Apprenticeships might last as long as seven years for some trades.

DIRT BOX

Seventeenth-century people were used to strong smells. It was quite normal to take a bath just three times a year, and people would go to the toilet right outside their back doors, in cellars, or even in fireplaces.

When Charles II (Charles I's son) and his court left Oxford in 1665, where they'd gone to escape the plague, they left behind:

... their excrements in every corner, in chimneys, studies, coal-houses, cellars.

A PEW TOO FEW

In the villages everyone knew their place - at least they were meant to. At the top was the squire, who was one of the gentry, then came a few rich farmers and lesser gentry and the parson, then some less well-off farmers and tradesmen. At the bottom were the landless labourers and servants.

Where you sat in church said a lot about who you were. Arguments about who sat where were common. Churches made money out of selling or renting space on pews.

COMMON LOGIC

At that time quite a lot of land wasn't owned by anyone in particular. Villagers had the right to graze their animals and to collect firewood on this common land. Many poor families, desperate for somewhere to live, built small cottages on it and on  other waste land. They even carved out small farms for themselves. These people were called 'squatters'. They were poor but free: they didn't have to work for the gentry and rich farmers.

Many of the gentry hated squatters. Wherever possible they enclosed the commons with hedges to make fields for sheep - there was money in wool. The poor were a threat to their power. As one hard-hearted land owner put it:

The poor increase like flies and lice, and these vermin will eat us up unless we enclose ...

A FESTIVE TIME WAS HAD BY ALL

From the point of view of the seventeenth-century gentry, life in a village must sometimes have seemed like life on the rim of a volcano. Down below was an unruly rabble with nothing much to lose, who might get out of control at any moment.

The rabble *did* get out of control - frequently. Throughout the year there were traditional festivals, when men and women could let off steam. There were 'wakes', held to celebrate the founding of churches, 'church ales 🦶', Mayday, Plough Monday, Harvest Home and a host of others, often local to an area. What the revellers got up to varied according to the festival, but mostly it involved a lot of drinking and dancing:

drinking

putting on traditional
Robin Hood plays

singing

eating

dancing round maypoles

Church ales were very common. All churches had their own beer-dispensing equipment.

Morris dancing

boxing

cudgel play

running races

KEEPING A LID ON IT

All too often, in fact usually, such festivities ended in drunkenness and fighting. When the innocent-looking morris dancers of Malmesbury visited Long Newton in Wiltshire on Plough Monday, 1641, they bellowed at the poor Newtonians:

Come three score 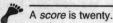 of you. You are but boys to we!

Several were badly injured in the fight between dancers and villagers which followed. But then, as the saying went:

Tis no festival unless there be some fightings.

A *score* is twenty.

18

No wonder many of the gentry wanted to keep a lid on it all. There was a whipping post in every village. Unfortunately, or fortunately depending on your point of view, they had another weapon - *Puritanism*. Puritanism was a strict form of Christianity which became very popular in the seventeenth century. What better way to tame the poorer classes than to make them go to church and listen to long, boring sermons in the hope of a better life in heaven?

Writing later, one old Puritan remembered that before 1640 anyone religious was:

... made the derision of the vulgar rabble ... the rest were dancing on the lord's day (Sunday).

Ha! The Puritans would put a stop to all that. Quite a few of the gentry and richer farmers and merchants became Puritans during the reign of Charles I. There were plenty in Parliament. By 1644, when Parliament had started to win the Civil War, a new law stated that even beggars and vagabonds had to go to church on Sundays.

Religion was very, very important to people in the seventeenth century. Men were prepared to fight and die over things which seem quite small today: over which prayer book to use or where to put the altar in

Roman Catholics were led by the Pope, who lived in Rome. The English (all except Catholics) thought that Catholicism was an evil empire bent on world domination. England's old enemies, France and Spain, were Catholic, so the English thought that British Catholics were little better than traitors. This was especially tough on the Irish: they *weren't* British but they *were* Catholic.

> I THINK CHURCH SERVICES SHOULD BE IN LATIN.

> MY CHURCH IS LED BY PRIESTS, BISHOPS, CARDINALS AND THE POPE.

> I BELIEVE THAT THE BREAD AND WINE OF HOLY COMMUNION TURN INTO THE ACTUAL FLESH AND BLOOD OF CHRIST.

> I LIKE RELIGIOUS PAINTINGS, STATUES AND INCENSE.

church. The Civil War was as much a war about religion as about who should run the country.

The three major Christian groups in the country were Roman Catholics, moderate Protestants and Puritans.

Protestants were part of a break-away movement from the Catholic Church which started in Northern Europe in the fifteenth century. Its followers were called *Protestants* because they *protested* about how things were done in the Catholic Church. The *Church of England* was Protestant but not very Protestant. It had bishops (but no Pope) and it allowed crucifixes, statues of saints, religious paintings, stained glass windows - and lots of festivals. Charles was a Church of England Protestant.

Puritans were Protestants with knobs on. Puritans believed in a stricter, purer form of Christianity (as they saw it) - hence the name. They were determined to stamp out anything which they thought was ungodly.

I DISAPPROVE OF FESTIVALS.

I FROWN ON BISHOPS, CROSSES, RELIGIOUS STATUES, AND PAINTINGS, STAINED GLASS WINDOWS, THE POPE (NATURALLY), LATIN (THE LANGUAGE OF THE DEVIL BECAUSE IT'S USED BY CATHOLICS).

PLAIN, SIMPLE CLOTHES

PURIFY THIS PROTESTANT

You're a Puritan. You think your Protestant friend has got Catholic tendencies. Can you strip him of the things you don't agree with? (Answers on page 122.)

LAST OF THE LITTER

To be blunt - a runt

Baby talk

Charles I was born on 19 November 1600 near Edinburgh in Scotland, where his father James was king. The custom was to wrap newborn babies in bandages, known as swaddling clothes. The bandages were wound tightly so that the babies couldn't move arms, legs or head. It was thought that unswaddled babies might tear off their ears, scratch out their eyes or even break their legs. Charles was a sickly little baby, but he survived being swaddled.

There was another reason for swaddling. Modern research has shown that swaddled babies sleep more, cry less and can be hung up on pegs, out of the way.

AND BABY WALK

Up to the age of three, Charles couldn't walk because his legs were too weak to support him. James suggested putting his legs in irons, but Charles' nurse wouldn't agree to it. James also suggested cutting the ligament at the base of Charles' tongue so as to cure his stammer, but fortunately the nurse resisted that suggestion also.

As it was, Charles grew up normal - but tiny. When fully grown he was only around 1.6 metres tall (5ft 3 in).

HANDSOME HENRY HANDS IN THE TOWEL

In 1603, the mighty Queen Elizabeth I of England died and James inherited her throne, thus becoming King of England as well as King of Scotland. Charles was only three at the time, and he wasn't expected to become king himself when James died. He was the baby of the

---

Ligaments are short, stringy bits of the body, used for connecting muscles or bones.

family and had an elder brother, the dashing Prince Henry. It was Henry whom everybody expected to be the next king. Henry was clever, good-looking and an athlete, whereas Charles was just a bit, well - ordinary.

Then, in August 1612, Henry fell dangerously ill 🦴. Among other treatments, the doctors smeared his body with meat from freshly killed cocks and pigeons.

Nothing worked. In November, they gave him a medicine made by the famous old adventurer, Sir Walter Raleigh.

SIR WALTER'S RECIPE

Pearl, musk, hartshorn, bezoarstone, mint, borage, gentian, mace, sugar, aloes and spirits of wine.

Henry died on 12 November.

 The illness was probably typhoid which is usually caught from drinking dirty water. Symptoms include: fever, loss of appetite, a cough, a headache and constipation.

HEIR STYLES

Twelve-year-old Charles was now heir to the throne, although he was definitely second best compared to his wonderful elder brother. Apart from being small and having a stammer, he just wasn't the type. Charles didn't have enough *charm* to be king. Throughout his life few people ever felt that he really *liked* them. He was too polite and too serious. On top of that, when he was young he was painfully shy and he used to blush a lot.

Charles' personality didn't matter so much while he was still a prince. Later, it was a disaster.

SPARE THE ROD AND SPOIL THE CHILD

In the seventeenth century young children were thought of as being a bit like animals. They had to be broken in like a foal or a puppy. Most school children were beaten until they bled on a regular basis. It was thought to be good for them, even though, as the philosopher John Locke remarked:

Why does Latin and Greek need the rod ... children learn to dance and fence without a whipping.

Being a prince, Charles didn't suffer as badly as some, but he was still expected to be incredibly respectful to his parents. In the seventeenth century, it was normal for children to kneel before their parents when greeting them or saying goodbye. Even grown-up sons had to keep their hats off in their parents' presence and grown-up daughters had to kneel or stand whenever their mothers were sitting. It was even worse if your father was James I. James had written a little book, *Basilikon Doron*, about how kings, like fathers, were given their power by God - the Divine Right of Kings in other words.

Small wonder that Charles, in his turn, grew up believing in the Divine Right of Kings.

Posh prince pursues petite princess

Charles grew up to be very different to his father.

James was ugly, badly-dressed and argumentative, with a very broad Scots accent - but clever.

Charles was better looking, well dressed, very polite, rather posh in fact, with a less strong Scots accent - and not so clever.

In 1624 this posh prince set out to woo Henrietta Maria, the fourteen-year-old daughter of the king of France. The French king chose to ignore the rumours that Charles was a bit of a weed.

Charles was small but Henrietta was *tiny*. Her head would barely reach his shoulder - once she met him. Not that she met him immediately. Charles' wooing was done by his 'Wooing Ambassador', an English lord who travelled to Paris in his place. Strangely, Charles still didn't meet her when he married her in March of the following year! A French Duke stood in for him at the ceremony outside the Cathedral of Notre Dame in Paris.

That was their first marriage. They had a second one in England a month later. But between the French wedding and the English wedding, James died. By the time of the English re-run, Charles and his very young bride had become king and queen of England and Scotland. And the stage was set for the tragedy which would follow.

PROBLEMS WITH PARLIAMENT

WHO'S BOSS?

KING AT LAST

Like James, Charles based his court in England which was by far the richer and more important of his two kingdoms. And he set out to rule as James had taught him to - like a king chosen by God. He didn't want anyone else telling him what to do. Since God had chosen him to rule, everybody had better obey him. He needed money - well, Parliament must cough up. Only Parliament could legally raise new taxes.

Parliament *did* cough up, but only for a while and only a bit. Parliament liked to be talked to politely. It didn't care for the sort of bluster that Charles went in for, as in this speech to Parliament in 1628:

... take not this as threatening for I scorn to threaten any but my equals ...

By that time, Parliament and King were about as friendly as a pair of Rottweilers with one bone between them. Charles was unwise to be so rude - as we've seen, the English king needed the willing help of the gentry, who were represented by Parliament, if he was to rule successfully.

Charles became involved in expensive wars, first against Spain (1625-30), then against France (1626-29) and finally against his own Scottish subjects (1639-40).

BLACK ROD BUNGLES IT

The problems between Charles and Parliament came to a head in 1629.

On 2 March, fed up with being criticised, Charles ordered the Speaker of the House of Commons to declare the House closed, to 'adjourn it' to use the correct expression.

Angry members of Parliament refused to obey. They held the Speaker down in his chair. The Speaker broke into tears.

While the Speaker was held down, members of Parliament passed resolutions against the King's government amid general uproar.

The King sent his royal guard to close the House. Black Rod , his official from the House of Lords, knocked on the door but was refused entry.

The *Speaker* of the House of Commons is elected by the members and keeps order in the debates. The first Speaker was elected in 1377.

As part of the opening ceremonies for every new parliament from that day to this, Black Rod knocks on the door and is refused entry. This symbolises the independence of the House of Commons.

When the politicians at last went home, Charles ordered the arrest of their leaders, whom he described as 'vipers'.

Parliament was closed. It stayed closed for the next eleven years.

MONEY, MONEY, MONEY

Now at last Charles could rule as he wanted to. There were no more piffling politicians to get in the way. His one problem was money, or rather, the lack of it. As we've seen, only Parliament could legally raise new taxes - and Parliament wasn't there any more. For the next eleven years, Charles scratched around for money as best he could:

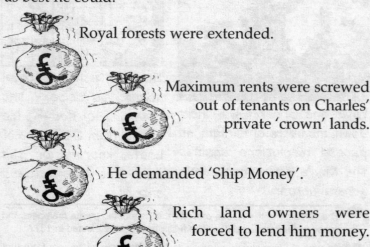

Royal forests were extended.

Maximum rents were screwed out of tenants on Charles' private 'crown' lands.

He demanded 'Ship Money'.

Rich land owners were forced to lend him money.

Ship Money was especially unpopular. English kings had had the right to raise money for the navy from sea ports for centuries, but Charles tried to extend this so that he could raise 'Ship Money' from inland towns as well. His version had nothing to do with ships. To all intents and purposes it was a new tax - but without Parliament's approval. This was very serious: if the king could raise taxes without Parliament, there would be no need for Parliaments at all. A rich land owner called John Hampden refused to pay and was sent to prison.

PRAISE THE LAUD - AND GET READY THE AMMUNITION

In 1633 Charles appointed a new Archbishop of Canterbury . The man he chose was William Laud (pronounced 'lord'). Laud was a disaster waiting to happen. He was a fussy, rude, cross little man, and a bit of a prig. He once told the students at Oxford:

... not to wear long hair, nor any boots, nor double stockings rolled down or hanging loose about their legs, as the manner of some slovens is.

The *Archbishop of Canterbury* is the head of the Church of England.

Charles and Laud agreed about religion. They were both straightforward Church of England men - Protestants in fact (see page 21). On the one hand they thought that the Catholic Church was a tyranny, and on the other hand they thought that Puritanism was a recipe for total chaos. They looked for a middle way.

Catholics weren't part of the Church of England, but plenty of Puritans still belonged to it. Puritanism is, after all, an extreme form of Protestantism. Laud set out to stamp on them. He called Puritanism a 'wolf to be held by the ears'. Among other things, he ordered that all altars should be placed at the east end of churches, not in the middle where Puritans liked them to be, and insisted that the official prayer book should be used in church services.

Puritans throughout Great Britain were outraged. Especially Scottish Puritans. When one of Laud's bishops tried to use the official Church of England prayer book in St Giles Cathedral, Edinburgh, he was hunted through the streets by a pack of three hundred furious women.

STEEPLE PEOPLE

The Church of England grew out of the hard-headed politics of sixteenth-century England, striking a middle road between extreme Catholicism and Puritanism so as to keep the country together.

1534: Act of Supremacy. Henry VIII breaks with the Roman Catholic Church.

1549: First prayer book to be printed in English, not Latin, prepared by Thomas Cranmer for Protestant Edward VI.

1553: 'Bloody' Catholic Queen Mary comes to the throne and tries to make England Catholic again. Many Protestant martyrs burned, including Thomas Cranmer.

1571: Thirty-nine Articles approved by moderate Protestant Elizabeth I, in which the doctrines of the Church of England are written out in such a way as to be acceptable to many Catholics as well as to Protestants.

1611: 'Authorized Version' of the Bible completed for King James I (& VI of Scotland).

THE FIRST BISHOPS' WAR

In 1639, Charles raised an army and marched off to punish the measly, disobedient Scottish Puritans.

His army was badly paid, badly led, badly trained and thoroughly disobedient itself.

On the way north the men murdered two of their officers who were Catholics.

AAAARRRGGGHHHHH!!!!

Scottish Highland armies were terrifying. The Highlanders would charge in a wedge-like formation, screaming horribly, then drop to one knee and stab upwards with their short swords .

As soon as the Scottish cannon were fired, Charles' English army threw down their weapons and ran away.

This tactic was first perfected by Roman legionaries.

THE SHORT AND THE LONG OF IT

Losing the Bishops' War was a big set-back for Charles. It made him look stupid. By April 1640, he was desperately short of money again, due to the cost of the war. He was forced to call his first parliament for eleven years. This parliament was led by a man called John Pym, nicknamed the 'Ox' because he was so rough and shaggy looking. The parliament refused to raise any money at all - not unless Charles changed his ways. It's called the Short Parliament because it lasted just three weeks before Charles closed it down.

Charles had raised no money and he'd made a new enemy: Pym. It was no coincidence that Pym became leader of the Parliamentarians during the first part of the Civil War.

But Charles still needed money to fight the Scots. He had no choice but to call another parliament. This new parliament, which met in November of 1640, had roughly the same people in it as the last one and it was even *more* bolshy. It's called the Long Parliament because it lasted, technically speaking, for twenty years - right through the time of the Civil War and beyond.

TIME RUNNING OUT

By now, power was slipping from Charles' fingers. Parliament had stood up to him - and forced him to back down. The Long Parliament charged Archbishop Laud and the King's leading statesman, the Earl of Strafford, with treason although all they'd really done was to obey their King.

Strafford was the King's new right-hand man. He was tough as old leather and he was the only man in the King's government who got things done. As far as Parliament was concerned, he was too dangerous to be allowed to live. As one Puritan Lord put it:

Stone dead hath no fellow.

Meaning, if Strafford was dead his supporters would have no one to gather round.

Strafford's trial took place in Westminster Hall and Charles listened from a little room behind the throne, shielded by a curtain. The crowd showed no respect for their king. They ate picnics and passed beer and wine around just as if he wasn't there.

Treason is serious disloyalty to a ruler, whether a king or a parliament. Over the years this has included pretty much any behaviour the accusers have wanted it to include.

Strafford was brave and answered his accusers so fearlessly that eventually the trial was abandoned. Parliament had to pass a special 'Act of Attainder' sentencing him to death without trial.

In May 1641 Strafford was beheaded - and Charles had signed the death warrant. He hoped that by doing so he would make better friends with Parliament.

THE BIRDS HAVE FLOWN

Leaders have to command the respect of the people they lead. Charles had lost the respect of his people. Power and popularity began to slip from his hands.

In the streets of London, Puritan preachers, often common tradesmen, urged the people to resist Archbishop Laud's reforms of the church.

Revolution was in the air. Both gentry and the nobles

were jostled in the streets of London. As one observer put it:

The present hatred of the citizens was such unto gentlemen ... that few durst come into the city.

There were brawls and fights in the streets and several people were killed.

TAKE THAT, YOU RASCALLY ROUNDHEAD!

Something had to be done. So Charles appointed Captain Thomas Lunsford to be the new chief of the Tower of London. Chief of the Tower was about as near as London came to a chief of police in those days.

Unfortunately, Lunsford was a thug. He was said to roast the flesh of babies. With other Royalist thugs, all with drawn swords, he terrorised Parliament for several days and threatened to cut the throats of Puritans.

Royalists were supporters of the King, see page 6.

Parliament demanded that Lunsford be sacked. The man was a menace. Reluctantly Charles agreed, losing yet more respect for changing his mind.

Charles then decided on a desperate last attempt to regain control of the situation. He would *force* Parliament to respect him - in person - by arresting its leading members. He was egged on by the queen. 'Go you poltroon! Go and pull those rogues out by the ears or never see my face again!' she told him.

Kings weren't meant to behave like this; it was against tradition and against the law. Charles marched to the House of Commons at the head of four hundred armed men to demand the arrest of five members: John Pym the 'Ox', John Hampden who had refused to pay ship money back in 1637, and three others, Denzil Holles, William Strode and Arthur Haselrig.

Polite as always, Charles took off his hat when he entered the Commons and sat down in the Speaker's chair.

But the five members had managed to slip out before he arrived.

'I see all my birds have flown,' Charles remarked quietly.

That was on 4 January 1642. Charles' gamble had failed. On 10 January, he left London, fearing for the life of his wife who, as a French Roman Catholic, was in extra danger from the mob. Their coach had to force its way through angry crowds.

The game was up.

WAR!

THE CUT AND THRUST OF ARGUMENT

Methinks the proverb should not be forgot
That wars are sweet to them that know them not.[*]

STANDARD PROCEDURE

In the months following their flight from London, the royal family scattered. Queen Henrietta Maria fled to Holland with the crown jewels, hoping to sell them to raise money for Charles. Charles made his way slowly northwards.

FAREWELL, MY LOVE.

That summer a last feeble attempt to patch up the quarrel between King and Parliament sputtered out because neither side was prepared to give way. Then on 22 August 1642, Charles raised his Royal Standard in the City of Nottingham, summoning men to join his

 John Taylor, 1642.

army to fight the forces of Parliament, based in London. That moment is said to have signalled the start of the Civil War. Twenty men were needed to carry the long, red pole, which was planted in a shallow hole, dug with knives. The standard blew over in a strong wind soon after - a bad omen.

JOINED UP FIGHTING

Nobody wanted a civil war, but all over England men drilled on patches of open land. The air was electric with excitement and danger. Castles were patched up and sentries were placed outside city walls, in case of sudden attack.

Communities and families were split down the middle depending on their political opinions, some men supporting Parliament and others the King. Tempers flared. In Gloucester a Puritan vicar who supported Parliament pulled the hair of a local constable and kicked him into a ditch. The constable was collecting money for the King. That was typical.

Rumour said that a troop of 'virtuous maidens' had been formed in Norwich to defend fellow women and to take revenge on Catholics and Cavaliers.

The men joined up for all manner of reasons, not all of them good.

Butchers were thought to make the best recruits because they were used to the sight of blood.

Some men were simply after excitement. They looked forward to plunder and pillage and having a really good time. One poem gives the reasons of a country yokel:

I will sell my chest and eke my plough
And get a sword if I know how,
And each man means to be right
I will swear and drink and roar ...

ON THE MARCH

By mid-September Charles and his army left the north of England and marched to Shrewsbury in the west of England to gather more recruits from Wales.

PIKE, AN ASHPOLE UP TO 5·5 METRES (18 FEET) LONG, WITH AN IRON TIP. THEY TENDED TO VIBRATE IF CARRIED HORIZONTALLY. SOME SOLDIERS CUT THEM SHORTER FOR EASIER MARCHING - AND PAID FOR IT LATER WITH THEIR LIVES.

INFANTRY MEN CARRIED AROUND 25 KILOGRAMS (55 POUNDS) OF EQUIPMENT INCLUDING BODY ARMOUR, HELMETS, SWORDS AND KNAPSACKS.

STEEL HELMETS WERE CALLED 'POTS'.

A 'CANNON ROYAL' NEEDED SIXTEEN HORSES OR NINETY MEN TO PULL IT.

Seventeenth-century armies with all their equipment might straggle for miles on the terrible roads of the period.

ARMIES, WERE FOLLOWED BY 'LEAGUER LADIES' — MOSTLY WOMEN RELATED IN SOME WAY TO SOLDIERS.

MUSKETEERS USED THEIR SUPPORTS AS WALKING STICKS.

THERE WERE NO STRONG BOOTS FOR THE INFANTRY — JUST COW-HIDE SHOES.

MUSKET BOX

Muskets were loaded with gunpowder, which was made from saltpetre, a product from bird droppings and human urine 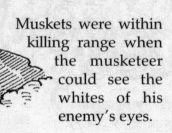.

Gunpowder was rammed down the barrel with a rod, the ball dropped on top of it and a wad of cloth was rammed on top to stop everything falling out.

A lit match cord was touched to the powder. Match cord was made of flax boiled in vinegar and soaked in saltpetre.

Muskets were within killing range when the musketeer could see the whites of his enemy's eyes.

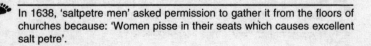
In 1638, 'saltpetre men' asked permission to gather it from the floors of churches because: 'Women pisse in their seats which causes excellent salt petre'.

BATTLE TACTICS

The start of a battle, when both armies were lined up facing each other, was perhaps the most terrifying time of all for soldiers, especially if they were new to war. Men were often allowed to get drunk so as to dull the fear.

The soldiers marched forward to the sound of fifes and drums. Parliamentary armies used to sing psalms as well.

Seventeenth-century generals had four types of force at their command: cavalry, pikes, musketeers, and cannon.

Cavalry would charge in a mass, so close together that their knees might touch. The sight of them was terrifying and often broke their opponents before the impact of the charge hit home. Then they lashed out with their swords - if their horses let them. The natural instinct of a horse is to avoid trouble.

Fifes are small, shrill flutes. (The Scots played bagpipes, but these had fallen out of fashion in England by the time of the Civil War.)

Psalms are ancient songs from the Bible.

Well-trained pikemen could stand up to cavalry. They might form circular 'hedgehogs' protected by stakes in the ground known as 'swines' feathers'.

Once the musketeers had fired their muskets and come to close quarters, they slugged it out with swords, axes, the butts of their guns and anything else that came to hand.

Cannon could be deadly. At the First Battle of Newbury in 1643 one officer saw:

...a whole file of men, six deep, with their heads struck off with one cannon shot of ours.

MURDER AT EDGEHILL

The first big battle of the war took place at Edgehill in Warwickshire on 23 October 1642. The battle lasted all afternoon and evening in bitterly cold weather. Nobody won, although perhaps Charles could have if he'd kept going the next day. Battles of the period were confused slogging matches. Each soldier's world closed down to a few metres of desperate violence, where all they could think about was to kill or be killed. Gun smoke often meant that men could only see a few metres in front of their faces, and armies would often try to get up wind of each other so that the smoke blew towards their enemies. At the Battle of Marston Moor in 1644 the powder smoke was:

... so thick that we saw no light, but what proceeded from the mouth of the guns.

At Edgehill, the men hacked and slashed until they could hack and slash no more. Then both armies drew back exhausted. They were so stunned by what they had done that they stayed on the field of battle through the night, too tired to move.

It was a dreadful, cold and frosty night. William Harvey, the discoverer of the circulation of blood, who was Charles' doctor, pulled a corpse over himself for warmth. The exhausted men could hear the groans of the dying being stripped of their clothes by plunderers out in the darkness between the two armies.

DON'T LOSE IT

It was the Duke of Wellington who said:

Nothing except a battle lost can be half so melancholy as a battle won.

When battles were over, prisoners and corpses were always stripped of nearly all their equipment and clothing. In the awful weather of the Civil War, clothes were almost more valuable than weapons.

It was often better to die quickly on the battlefield than to be wounded - most of the wounded died anyway: medical knowledge was very poor by modern standards. When Colonel Sandy was wounded in a skirmish a few weeks before Edgehill:

... in his thigh the flesh did daily rot and putrefy and was cut away by degrees even to bearing the bone naked, and stunk in so loathsome a manner that he was a burden to himself and his friends.

It was better to be taken prisoner, then at least you got the chance to change sides - although not if Charles had anything to do with it. One of Charles' battle cries in 1642 was:

God save King Charles and hang all Roundheads.

Parliamentary forces weren't that ruthless - unless the prisoner was an Irish Catholic. Puritans hated Irish Catholics because they were thought to be in league with England's Catholic enemies overseas. In October 1644 Parliament passed the shameful order:

... no quarter shall henceforth be given to any Irishman or Papist *born in Ireland captured on land or sea.*

Papist meant Catholic - a follower of the Pope.

THE PERFECT PIKEMAN

This pikeman has far too much equipment.
What should he keep?
(Answers on page 122.)

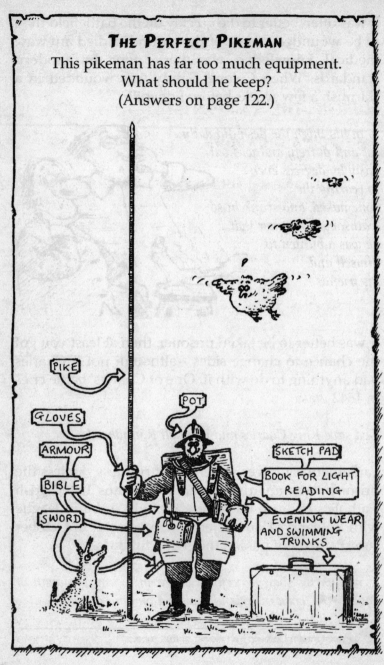

PIKE

GLOVES

ARMOUR

BIBLE

SWORD

POT

SKETCH PAD

BOOK FOR LIGHT READING

EVENING WEAR AND SWIMMING TRUNKS

BESIEGED!

RUN UP THE RAMPARTS!

TIME FOR A SHOWDOWN

While Charles was gathering men for his army in the north, Parliament had been left to rule the roost in London. Most of the citizens of London supported Parliament anyway. After Edgehill, Charles' army marched towards them for a final encounter. If he could beat London, the war was over.

But London was expecting him. The citizens had started to build their defences. 20,000 people per day laboured like ants on an earth wall which was 5.5 metres (18 ft) high and 18 kilometres (11 miles) round when it was finished. Everyone joined in, even a brigade of 'oyster wives'. There was a poem about them:

From ladies down to oyster wenches
Labour'd like pioneers in trenches,
Fell to their pick-axes and tools,
And helped the men to dig like moles.

The King's nephew and dashing young cavalry commander, Prince Rupert, spent a whole day disguised as a woman so as to examine London's new defences more closely. Broad-shouldered and nearly two metres (6ft 4 in) in his stockings, he must have looked pretty odd.

SIEGE TACTICS - AND TIPS FOR TOSSING IN THE TOWEL

The Civil War was a war of sieges  as well as battles in open country, because the countryside was still dominated by castles and walled towns as it had been in the Middle Ages.

Castles were held by their owners for whichever side they supported. Towns didn't have owners of course, but if most of the wealthy families in a town supported a particular side (often Parliament since rich merchants tended to be Puritans) they would probably win control of it. The opposition would then have to break in from outside.

 During a *siege* the attackers surround a castle or other fortified place and try to starve or beat it into surrender. Sieges can go on for weeks, sometimes even for years.

Sieges were often worse than battles - for defenders and attackers alike. Attackers had to camp outside in the rain and cold. Only officers had tents. Sometimes the conditions were so dreadful that the attackers gave up, as happened to the Roundhead soldiers when they besieged Manchester. They left:

... by reason of cold, wet, thirst and want of sleep.

For the defenders the big problem was deciding when to fight and when to surrender. The trick was to hold out for just the right length of time - surrender too soon and you might be arrested as a traitor by your own side - too slow and you might all be massacred. Massacre of those who failed to surrender was normal in those days. As the Royalist general Lord Byron explained after he had taken the Parliament-held town of Nantwich:

I put them all to the sword which I find is the best way to deal with these people, for mercy to them is cruelty.

The defenders fought back as best they could. They would sally out and attack the besiegers. At Worcester, Royalist Captain Hodgkins, known as 'Wicked Will', and a friend got blind drunk 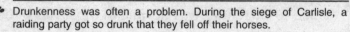 and sallied out against thirty enemy dragoons. They returned wounded but with seven prisoners.

Drunkenness was often a problem. During the siege of Carlisle, a raiding party got so drunk that they fell off their horses.

Dragoons were lightly-armed cavalry.

If the food and water ran out, the defenders had to give up. During the siege of Royalist Lathom House in Lancashire, the Roundhead attackers knew that the end was near by the vile smell of the defenders' clothes. There was no water left to wash them with.

TURN-AROUND AT TURNHAM

Meanwhile back outside London, Charles led his army towards the city. Thousands of citizens marched out of the city to block his advance. Almost everyone came, from members of Parliament down to humble apprentices. London's trained bands - part-time soldiers - were out in force. Together with the battered Parliamentary army which had fought at Edgehill, they positioned themselves behind hedges and other barriers at Turnham Green.

SIEGE TACTICS

For each correct answer climb five steps up the ladder. For each incorrect answer move three steps down.

(Answers at the bottom of the page.)

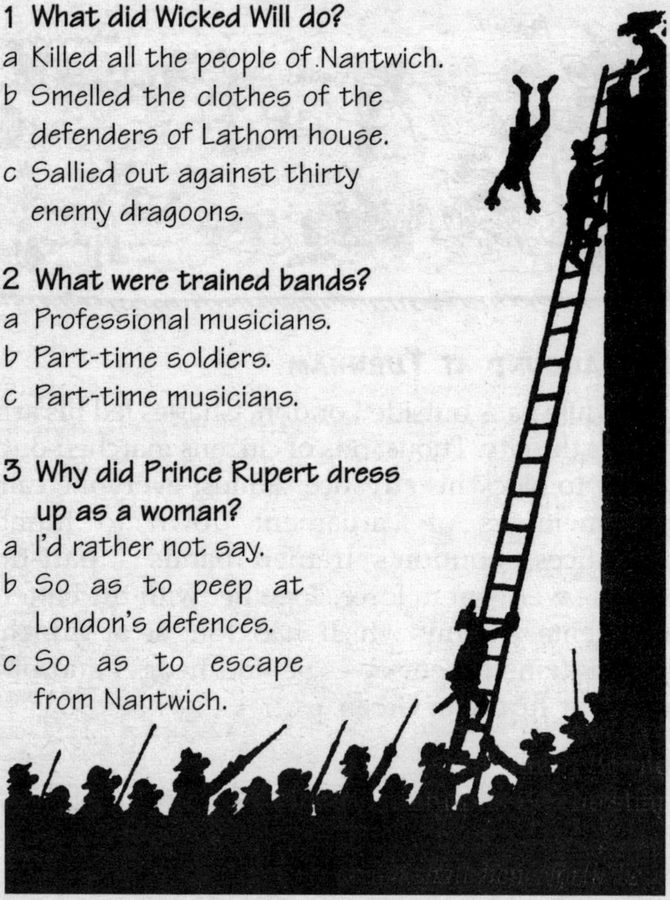

1 What did Wicked Will do?
a Killed all the people of Nantwich.
b Smelled the clothes of the defenders of Lathom house.
c Sallied out against thirty enemy dragoons.

2 What were trained bands?
a Professional musicians.
b Part-time soldiers.
c Part-time musicians.

3 Why did Prince Rupert dress up as a woman?
a I'd rather not say.
b So as to peep at London's defences.
c So as to escape from Nantwich.

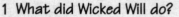

Answers: 1-c, 2-b, 3-b

A POX ON OXFORD

Turnham Green is the biggest might-have-been of the Civil War. If Charles had attacked there and then, he might well have captured London and won the war. But he didn't dare to use his cavalry because there were too many hedges. Instead, the Royalist army turned back towards Oxford.

Charles arrived in Oxford on 29 November 1642. And there he stayed. The town became his headquarters - a mad, bad, overcrowded sort of place, part Royal court and part army barracks . He set up court in Christ Church College, which was comfortable enough, but many of his lords and ladies had to take lodgings wherever they could find them:

... we came to a baker's house in an obscure street, and from rooms well furnished to lie in a very bad bed in a garret ...

 The Oxford townspeople would probably have sided with Parliament - if they had had a say in the matter. But Charles had an army and they didn't.

The crowds made for dirt and the dirt made for disease. To avoid infection many people walked the streets with their noses plugged with wormwood or holding pieces of tarred rope against them. Some even held up 'socks from sweating feet'.

Royalist Oxford was a dangerous place. The cavaliers were a rough bunch. As the Mayor of Sandwich complained later in the war:

... after spending the night at an inn, rather than paying they would rip up the feather beds and 'for sport' smash all the barrels of wine or beer they had not drunk.

As it was, in Oxford there was almost a duel a day between Cavalier officers. Prince Rupert had to part two of them with a pole axe.

Wormwood is a bitter herb, nowadays used as part of the flavouring of Vermouth, an alcoholic drink.

Ride on, Rupert

Prince Rupert was the best of Charles' generals. He was the son of Charles' sister Elizabeth, a beautiful woman who married a German ruler. She had a poem written about her in the years before the war started:

> *You meaner beauties of the night,*
> *That poorly satisfy our eyes*
> *More by your number than your light,*
> *You common people of the skies,*
> *What are you, when the Moon shall rise?*

Rupert was good-looking like his mother. He was also bad mannered, proud - and a brilliant soldier. He trained his cavalry to charge in close formation, their knees almost touching, and not to waste time in firing their pistols. They went in like a tank. In battle after battle Rupert's cavalry won the day - only to throw it all away by rushing off to loot the enemy baggage train.

 To 'His Mistris' by Sir Henry Wotton.

Rupert was brilliant. However, unfortunately for Charles, Parliament had a brilliant soldier of its own who was also a cavalry commander. And their soldier wasn't just brilliant, he was a military genius. When questioning a Parliamentary prisoner before a battle in Yorkshire, Rupert was heard to ask one question with special interest:

Is Cromwell there?

GODLY MEN ✞ AND MAD MEN

HOW TO MIX POLITICS AND RELIGION

ENTER THE SLOVEN

Oliver Cromwell, Parliament's brilliant cavalry commander, was a country squire from East Anglia. He was big, but no beauty:

... his linen was plain and not very clean ... his stature of good size, his sword stuck close to his side; his countenance swollen and reddish; his voice sharp and untunable ...

Cromwell was shabby, but there was something about him which made people sit up and take note. He seemed destined to be great. His cousin John Hampden was once asked by a man who had never seen Cromwell before: 'Who is that sloven?' Hampden replied:

... that sloven will be the greatest man in England.

Cromwell's strength came from his religious beliefs.

He was a straightforward Puritan and he believed he had a direct line to God. He always *knew* he was in the right:

You shall scarce speak to Cromwell about anything, but he will ... call God to record, he will weep, howl and repent - even while he doth smite you under the first rib.

IRONSIDES

Once the war started, Cromwell gathered a first class troop of cavalry for the Parliamentary army. They became known as the Ironsides . Cromwell picked honest, God-fearing men from East Anglia for his troop. He knew what he was doing:

I had rather have a plain russet-coated captain that knows what he fights for, and loves what he knows than that which you call a gentleman and nothing else.

Unlike most soldiers of the time, Ironsides weren't allowed to get drunk and they had to pay a twelve penny fine if they swore. They had iron discipline, so that whereas Rupert's men tended to disappear in

Prince Rupert coined the name 'Ironsides' for Cromwell after the Battle of Marston Moor in 1644, but the name was soon applied to the whole troop.

search of loot after a successful charge, the Ironsides would wheel round and charge their enemy from behind.

Later in the war, Parliament set up a new army modelled in many ways on Cromwell's Ironsides. The soldiers wore red coats and were properly disciplined and regularly paid: about ten (new) pence per day for a cavalry man and his horse, about eight (new) pence per day for infantry. It's claimed that this army, the 'New Model Army', was the first modern army in Europe.

VIRTUOUS VANDALS

Religion was all the rage in the Puritan Parliamentary army. Preachers would try to whip the Roundheads into a passion before battle. One preacher is described as:

... thrashing such a sweating sermon that he put off his doublet.

 The British army continued to wear red coats right until the end of the nineteenth century.

The Roundheads saw the existing Church of England as the enemy of true Puritan religion (see page 21). They thought it was little better than Catholicism. They stabled their horses in the churches and smashed up anything they thought was a bit Roman Catholic. Go to almost any English church or cathedral today and you will see their handiwork: faces of statues hacked off, plain glass windows where there was once stained glass, whole galleries of statues removed from the outsides of cathedrals.

In Rochester Cathedral they kicked rare books from the library across the floor and smashed the glass windows and the statues.

In Colchester they threw bones from tombs about.

In Worcester Cathedral they used the choir stalls as a toilet.

Not that all Roundheads were killjoys - it was said that soldiers sleeping in the Cambridge colleges demanded 'fiddlers and revels by day and night'.

BASHER BOX

It was by no means only Roundhead soldiers who smashed up churches. William 'Basher' Dowsing was an ordinary Roundhead who was specially employed to smash up the churches of East Anglia. Basher was proud of his work and kept a detailed record. He's described as going at it with a long pole:

... like a bedlam [madman] breaking glasse windowes.

ELECT SECTS

Many Parliamentary soldiers joined extreme religious sects either during the war or soon after it. Most of these sects believed that their members were the 'elect' (chosen) of God and would be saved when Christ returned, which might happen at any time. Then the 'saints', i.e. themselves, would inherit the Earth for a thousand years.

Common to all these sects was the idea that each of us can hear the voice of God within us if we listen hard

A *sect* is a small group of believers with their own special opinions about a religion.

enough. In its most extreme form this meant that there was no need for priests, for the Bible or even for prayer.

Muggletonians spoke (or preached?) against prayer and preaching.

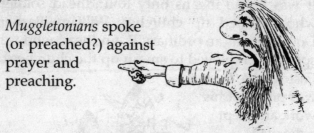

Grindletonians (named after the village of Grindleton where the sect started) believed that 'the assured Christian can never commit a gross sin' - which was rather convenient.

Fifth Monarchists believed that there had already been four monarchies: Assyrian, Persian, Greek and Roman. When Christ returned he would rule for a thousand years and that would be the Fifth Monarchy. Fifth Monarchists were revolutionaries. At one of their gatherings they voted that 'God's people must be a bloody people'.

Adamites preached naked because Adam and Eve had gone naked in the Garden of Eden in the Bible.

Anabaptists believed in adult baptism, not baptism of children and infants. 'Anabaptist' became a general term of abuse for extreme sectarians.

Ranters ranted. They deserve a special section.

Quakers quaked. They deserve a special section too.

RANTERS

Ranters were very extreme sectarians, although some of their opinions were shared by others. Their own name for themselves was 'My One Flesh'. They believed that all people are equal and called each other 'fellow creature' as a greeting.

Swearing was meant to be an upper class habit in those days. (The Cavaliers were called 'Dammees'.) However, if common people were caught swearing, they might be fined or even have a hole bored through the tongue. So Ranters took to swearing with a vengeance, just to show they could. Abiezer Coppe was said to have sworn for an hour continuously in the pulpit, howling:

A pox of God take all your prayers.

Ranters took the idea that each person can hear the voice of God to an incredible extreme:

Those are most perfect ... which do commit the greatest sins with least remorse ...

Nothing was a sin if God told you to do it. If any belief was a license to let you hair down, this was it! One Ranter claimed that drunkenness helped him to see God better! The Ranters smoked tobacco and drank beer at their meetings. They sang, whistled, danced and talked a lot - 'ranted' in other words. One woman took to telling members of Parliament that murder, adultery and theft weren't sins at all.

Adultery is when a married man or woman gets together with someone he or she isn't married to.

In fact, it seemed that some Ranters hardly even believed in God. When John Boggis was asked to say thanks to God before a meal, he replied:

To whom shall I give thanks, to the butcher, or to the bull, or to the cow?

MADNESS!

Ranting proved very attractive to men who can only be described as mad.

Thomas Tany believed that God had ordered him to kill members of Parliament. He attacked with a rusty sword and wounded a door keeper. He also burned the Bible.

Arise Evans wasn't an official Ranter but he was of the same ilk. He claimed to have flown and was imprisoned for saying that he was Christ. He also claimed to be a prophet but people tended to collapse with laughter when he prophesied.

Abiezer Coppe protested against rich men's coaches, 'leaping, skipping and dancing like one of the fools':

> *... howl, howl ye nobles, howl honourable, howl ye rich men for the miseries that are coming upon you*

Such men weren't much use to the Parliamentary army, not if they thought like Coppe towards the end of the war:

> *We (holily) scorn to fight for anything; we had as lief be dead drunk every day of the week ...*

 Prophets can foresee the future.

ARE YOU MAD?

Now's your chance to find out.
(Answers on page 123.)

1 Your Member of Parliament has knocked on your door, canvassing for support in the next election. Do you:

a Kill him?
b Ask him in for a cup of tea?
c Keep the door closed and make a deep barking noise, so that he thinks you're a fierce dog and goes away?

2 What do you do if you see a Rolls Royce?
a Ignore it.
b Ask the owner for his or her autograph in case they're a celebrity.
c Skip and dance in front of it.

3 What are you?
a Jesus Christ.
b Napoleon.
c The person whose name is written in your passport.

4 You've run out of fuel for the fire. Do you:
a Saw up the bannisters and burn them instead?
b Tear up the family Bible and burn it?
c Wrap up warm and wait for the shops to open tomorrow?

QUAKERS

Quakers wouldn't have been much more use to the army than Ranters, not after they became pacifists . As it was, they refused to obey officers unless they agreed with their orders and they made it clear that they didn't really intend to kill anyone. Their proper name was *The Society of the Friends of Truth* (nowadays just *The Society of Friends*) and they're the only seventeenth-century sect which is still going today.

Quakers were difficult to get along with in the early days. They were founded by George Fox, the son of a weaver. Fox looked down on Ranters because he thought they scraped and bowed too much to the upper classes. When greeted politely by a Ranter, Fox replied:

Repent thou swine and beast!

Quakers were either admired or hated depending on your point of view. The more extreme among them preached naked, foamed at the mouth and wore ashes on their heads.

Pacifists think it's wrong to fight in wars.

All of them heckled in church services.

They refused to bow down or take their hats off to anyone.

What is most impressive about them is how they allowed themselves to be beaten and slung in prison time and again, never losing their courage - and usually preaching at their poor tormentors, until their tormentors were glad to be rid of them.

Fox Box

George Fox, the founder of Quakerism, wandered up and down England recruiting thousands to his cause. He lived rough, sleeping in ditches and under hedges when night fell.

His hair was uncut and straggled down his back 'like rats tails' and he wore the leather doublet and breeches of a common labourer. His white hat was on his head for one reason only - so as *not* to take it off in the presence of ladies and gentlemen! He seems to have been totally without fear and suffered many, many beatings. He was first imprisoned in 1649 for brawling in church.

WIVES AND WITCHES

WHAT WOMEN GOT UP TO IN THE WAR

For most of history most ordinary women (and indeed most men) have been in the background. They've got on with their lives, tending to their families and children, and they've hardly made a ripple on the surface of the pond. But in the revolutionary fever of the 1640s and 1650s that started to change.

BUT FIRST - MRS NORMAL

Not that being married 🐾 and tending to your family was an easy option. There were no easy options. During the seventeenth century, women were still very much under the control of their husbands and the law made sure they stayed that way. Punishments for women who were unfaithful or were thought to nag their husbands included the scold's bridle, which must have been extremely painful and uncomfortable, and often the ducking stool, which was quite dangerous.

NO STOOL FOR US THOUGH!

Some sectarians (members of a sect), as extreme Puritans were called, such as Thomas Tany, thought that marriage was: 'a very wicked thing'.

Despite the horrors of the ducking stool and scold's bridle, it's clear that many marriages were happy and that husbands and wives were often very much in love with each other. The dangers of war only made them love more deeply. Elizabeth Bourchier wrote to her husband, the Earl of Rutland, who was off fighting:

Oh my heart, so you were safe I did not care if I were dead ... for God's sake write to me and come as soon as you can.

FIGHTING FEMALES

Elizabeth Bourchier finished her letter: 'Your dutiful and obedient wife and humble servant'. This didn't mean that she loved him less, but it shows that women, for all their bravery, were a long way from seeing themselves as equal to men.

Which was a shame because the women of the Civil War were often very brave. Some even dressed up as soldiers so as to stay with their husbands - or simply so as to join in the fighting.

Several noble ladies took charge of the defence of the family castle while their husbands were off fighting and some of the fiercest defenders in sieges were women:

Lady May Bankes and her daughters, plus five soldiers, threw burning embers and stones on to the heads of the attacking Roundheads at Corfe Castle.

Dorothy Hazard and her friends filled up a breach in the wall with sandbags during the siege of Bristol. They then took up position behind the guns to make sure the men fired properly.

During the siege of Chester, the women shot from walls, windows and rooftops. They were described as:

... all on fire, storming in gallant emulation to outdo our men.

... AND PEACE WOMEN

As the war continued, more and more people got fed up with the whole business. In 1643 a crowd of peace women wearing white ribbons demonstrated outside

Parliament. They banged on the doors and attacked members trying to leave. When soldiers fired blanks at them to make them go away, they scoffed:

Nothing but powder!

Finally the demonstration was broken up by mounted soldiers and one woman's nose was chopped of.

QUAKER LADIES

Some of the extreme Puritan sects, such as the Quakers, decided that they were against fighting on principle, although this happened towards the end of the fighting or after it was all over. The glory days of the Quaker women came after the war, but they deserve a mention here because they show how the war changed the way some women thought about themselves. Quaker women were as outrageous as their men and every bit as brave.

Elizabeth Hooton went to the West Indies where she stood up for the rights of the black slaves. In New England she was whipped, sent into the wilds, returned and was whipped to the point of losing her skin. She drove her tormentors to distraction because she never stopped badgering them. Back in England, after the war was over, she preached at easy-going Charles II.

Mary Fisher started life as a servant in Yorkshire. After whippings and the threat of execution while making converts in America, she set out to convert the Muslim Sultan of Turkey, the arch-enemy of Christian Europe. The Sultan was on his way to attack Vienna when she caught up with him and his army. Ushered into his tent, she preached fearlessly for a long time. When she'd finished, the Sultan offered her an escort to his capital of Constantinople (modern Istanbul). Mary was eventually executed by fellow Christians in Boston, America.

Martha Simmonds went too far. She developed a horrible, buzzing way of singing in order to drown out men's voices at meetings. She would chant the same word for hours and hours.

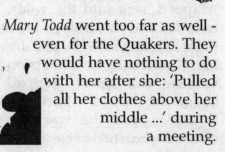

Mary Todd went too far as well - even for the Quakers. They would have nothing to do with her after she: 'Pulled all her clothes above her middle ...' during a meeting.

MORE MADNESS!

In the main, Quaker women were incredibly brave but they weren't mad. Other women went totally over the top.

Mary Adams got pregnant and believed that she was about to give birth to Christ. (She wasn't the only one.)

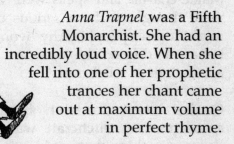

Anna Trapnel was a Fifth Monarchist. She had an incredibly loud voice. When she fell into one of her prophetic trances her chant came out at maximum volume in perfect rhyme.

Lady Eleanor Davies successfully prophesied the death or downfall of two husbands and spent time in a lunatic asylum. She once sat on the bishop's throne at Lichfield, poured hot tar and wheat paste on the altar cloth and declared herself Archbishop. She was described by an enemy as:

... abominable stinking great simnel face excrement .

 To translate: 'horrible, smelly, great cake-face poo'.

WHICH WOMAN IS A WITCH?

People believed in magic in the seventeenth century. It was believed that just a touch from the king could cure scrofula . And almost everyone believed in 'sympathetic magic': for instance, that bleeding from a wound could be stopped by wiping the weapon with a handkerchief soaked in the victim's blood.

Magic charms and spells were widely used. Witches were thought to be a serious danger because they might curse people. Any woman who looked or behaved differently was an obvious target for accusations of witchcraft.

Quaker women certainly behaved differently. An accusation of witchcraft was probably the most dangerous thing that could happen to them. During her trip to America, Mary Fisher and two other women were stripped naked and tormented for being witches. They were lucky to escape with their lives.

> LOOK! THAT WOMAN'S BEHAVING DIFFERENTLY. SHE MUST BE A WITCH!

> THAT'S NOT A WOMAN, THAT'S A HORSE.

Scrofula was probably a form of tuberculosis, a disease of the lungs.

In the fever of war many innocent victims were picked on by men such as Mathew Hopkins, the most famous witch-finder of the period. He captured several hundred so-called witches.

It's worth bearing in mind that all of the victims of men like Hopkins were totally innocent.

Unless of course you believe in witchcraft.

KING ESCAPES, SHOCK!

WHEREBY CHARLES GETS IN A PICKLE

STOP THE MADNESS!

By 1645 Charles was still based at Oxford, and London was still controlled by Parliament. The war had been going on for three years. A lot of people, perhaps most of them, just wanted the war to end and didn't care too much who won it. They were fed up with the soldiers of both sides. One countryman wrote a poem about it:

> I had six oxen the other day
> And them the Roundheads got away
> A mischief on them speed.
> I had six horses in the hole
> And them the Cavaliers stole.
> I think in this they are agreed.

No one could think of a way to stop the madness. Lord Essex, the top Parliamentary commander at the start of the war, once suggested that selected troops from each side should fight it out in a sort of grand duel.

More sensibly, some countrymen formed their own armed bands to fight off the soldiers of either side. These 'Clubmen' became quite a nuisance to both sides.

WHO DO YOU THINK YOU ARE?

War was crazy. It was understandable that the Clubmen were fed up with it. One of the craziest incidents happened just before the Battle of Naseby in 1645. The left and right wings of a Royalist troop commanded by Baron Goring mistook each other for the enemy. They fought for over an hour in 'the most fantastical accident since the war began', as Goring put it.

THE BATTLE OF NASEBY

At long last, on 14 June 1645, the New Model Army fought a major battle with the Royalists - at Naseby, south of Leicester. This turned out to be the deciding battle of the war, and it was the first time that Parliament's New Model Army fought a major battle.

The New Model Army was commanded by Thomas Fairfax, a youngish man with long black hair, known as 'Black Tom'.

The Royalist army was commanded by the king in person. Charles looked magnificent in full armour on a dashing horse.

The Royalists were outnumbered and less well-disciplined than the New Model Army. After a long hard struggle, they broke and fled. In those days, most soldiers were killed when running away, not when fighting. At the end of the day, Royalist bodies lay scattered over four miles of Leicestershire countryside 'but most thick on the hill'.

Royalist prisoners were taken to London where they were paraded through the streets.

Worst of all for Charles, his enemies captured his secret files and letters. In the past, as a good, Protestant, Church of England man, Charles had tried hard to defeat Irish Catholic rebels against his rule. The letters showed that he was now trying to arrange for a *Catholic* Irish army to invade England to support his own, Protestant English army. This was shocking news to all English Protestants and not just to Puritans.

Parliament published the letters, persuading many people that Charles could never ever be trusted. The letters did as much damage to Charles' cause as losing the Battle of Naseby.

THE SCARPER TO SCOTLAND

The war dragged on after Naseby but Charles' cause was lost. From then on, the Parliamentary forces scooped up castles and towns like squirrels picking up nuts. By March of the following year, Oxford itself was no longer safe. Charles left Oxford secretly on 27 April 1646 with two companions, disguised as their servant.

FALSE BEARD

If Charles had been sensible he would have headed for the continent and safety. But Charles wasn't sensible. Despite everything that had happened to him, he still believed that as God's chosen ruler he was safe in his own country. He headed north and gave himself up to the Scots instead.

What is known as the First Civil War was over.

BORED TO TEARS

For the next nine months, Charles was the rather unwelcome guest of his Scottish subjects. The Scots were Presbyterians, an especially dour sort of Puritan and not at all like the mad sectarians of England. The Presbyterians wanted to set up one strict, well-organised Puritan Church run by 'elders ' which would be exactly the same all over Britain.

For nine months, one after another, hopeful Presbyterians tried to persuade Charles to fall in with their plans. They almost bored him into it. But Charles was still a Church of England man. He fended them off as best he could and played the odd game of golf to keep up his spirits. When the Scots finally passed him to his Parliamentary enemies ('sold' might be a better word), he seemed almost relieved.

GOLF! WHAT'S WRONG WITH THE BIBLE?

 Presbyter is Latin for an 'elder'. The Presbyterian Church would be led by the older, wiser men of the community.

BORED BUT NOT BEATEN

This king is being bored to tears by seventeenth-century Presbyterians. Some of them aren't all that they seem. Can you spot which ones? (Answer on page 123.)

DIGGING FOR VICTORY

REVOLUTION IS IN THE AIR

PRESBYTERIANS V. INDEPENDENTS

Parliament's troubles didn't end with the defeat of Charles. It was no longer a simple question of King against Parliament. No sooner had they won the war than the Roundheads began to quarrel among themselves.

Parliament itself was dominated by members of Parliament who were *Presbyterians*, like their Scottish neighbours. They wanted to get rid of the Church of England and set up a strict Presbyterian system in its place which would be the same all over England (see page 90).

The New Model Army was dominated by *Independents*. Independents believed in freedom of worship - that each little church in England should be free to worship as it chose. Some Independents even believed in freedom of worship for Catholics and Jews . Oliver Cromwell was an Independent.

The Jews had been expelled from England in the Middle Ages. It was Oliver Cromwell who allowed them back again a few years later.

Change your partners - Part 1

Over the following two years the English Civil War turned into a revolution in all but name. At times, events moved very fast indeed. People made friends, then ganged up on each other, then made friends again - and at the end of it all the King lost his head.

1. Parliament, dominated by *Presbyterians*, wanted to disband most of the New Model Army now that the war had been won. They feared that the Army, controlled by *Independents*, had grown too powerful.

2. Parliament made friends with the Scottish Presbyterians, so as to gang up on the New Model Army.

3. The Army started to make friends with the King(!) so that between them they could gang up on Parliament. The Army 'rescued' the King from Parliament (3 June 1647).

4. The Army refused to obey Parliament's order to disband - to break up and go home (10 June 1647). The soldiers were owed back-pay and had other complaints, such as no pensions for the wounded.

5. There were passionate arguments in the Army over how the country should be run. (September - November 1647.)

ELECTIONS EVERY TWO YEARS!

NO MORE PARLIAMENTS!

NO MORE KINGS!

NO MORE LORDS!

(Continued on page 106.)

PASS THE PARCEL

Charles was handed over to the control of Parliament by the Scots on 30 January 1647. By this time, the Independents in the New Model Army were worried that Parliament might persuade the King to help set up Presbyterianism in England - in return for getting his crown back.

On 1 June 1647, the Army pounced. George Joyce, a young officer in the New Model Army, cantered into the courtyard of Holdenby House where Charles was being held under the control of Parliament. Joyce had five hundred troopers with him and he was under orders to remove the King.

When Charles asked Joyce what authority he had, Joyce turned in his saddle and politely pointed at the men behind him.

The top Army commanders treated Charles rather better than the Scots or Parliament had done. Charles was allowed to live in Hampton Court Palace, just outside London, and had his former servants to wait on him.

Cromwell and his son-in-law, Henry Ireton, also a senior army commander, brought their wives to have dinner with him. Cromwell seems to have felt rather sorry for Charles at this time.

PUTNEY PROBLEMS

The problem for the New Model Army was: now that they'd got hold of the king, what were they meant to do with him? Cromwell and the other top men in the army were all for putting Charles back on his throne - under certain strict conditions. As one writer put it:

A crown so near lost was never so near won.

 But Charles had all the sense of a headless chicken. He wouldn't agree to anything. Meanwhile, revolution was in the air. Wild

preachers such as Praise-God Barebone 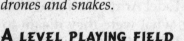 and his two brothers: Christ-Came-Into-The-World-To-Save Barebone and If-Christ-Had-Not-Died-Thou-Hadst-Not-Been-Saved Barebone demanded greater reforms.

The soldiers of the New Model Army elected 'agitators' to debate what to do next. They met in Putney Church just outside London. The discussions of the agitators are called the 'Putney Debates'. They started in October 1647 and went on for two months. The little church echoed with the voices of common soldiers as they argued passionately about the future of their country - watched by their officers, who mostly:

... sat still like so many drones and snakes.

A LEVEL PLAYING FIELD

Many soldiers belonged to a movement called the 'Levellers'. Levellers got their name because they were accused of wanting to level things off, to make the rich level with the poor. They argued that the lower classes were the truest followers of God and that the army

 Praise-God Barebone later became a leading member of the 'Barebones' Parliament of 1653. This was a short-lived Parliament dominated by Independents and by Oliver Cromwell.

should only use its power to hand power back to the common people. As one of their leaders, Colonel Rainsborough put it at Putney:

I think the poorest he that is in England has a life to lead as the greatest he ...

Some of their ideas seem very modern:

All adult men to have the right to vote in elections . (The idea of women voting didn't really occur for another two hundred years.)

All power to be held by the House of Commons, not by the King or the House of Lords.

Parliaments to be elected every one or two years.

Freedom of religion for all (well, almost all).

Some Levellers, including their leader John Lilburne, would have left out servants and the very poor.

99

DIGGERS

The Diggers were part of the English Revolution. They believed that all men should have 'an equal share in the earth'. There were several Digger communities. The most famous was set up by their leader, Gerrard Winstanley, in April 1649 on waste land on St George's Hill, Weybridge. The local Levellers wrote a pamphlet about the Digger community, *Light Shining in Buckinghamshire*, with a sequel, *More Light Shining in Buckinghamshire*.

The Diggers set to work to cultivate the waste land. Other poor people soon joined them and soon over a hundred Diggers were toiling away. Local landlords were outraged. They organised raiding parties and by the following year the Diggers of St George's Hill were forced to give up.

CLAMP DOWN

Where was it all leading to? Heavens, you might wake up and find a bunch of smelly beggars in your garden digging up the vegetables, if you weren't careful! Rich men were seriously worried by the Levellers and Diggers and all the mad sectarians. Cromwell, Fairfax and the other 'Grandees' of the Army, as they were called, decided to clamp down. Cromwell described the Levellers as:

a despicable and contemptible generation of men ... persons differing little from beasts ...

Fairfax cleverly arranged that the Putney Debates should continue at three separate meetings on three separate days. This divided up the soldiers. Two regiments who had kicked out their officers and were wearing green Leveller ribbons marched to the first meeting. Fairfax was waiting for them with loyal soldiers to back him up.

The ribbons were torn from their hats and they were forced at gun point to tear up copies of the Leveller pamphlet *Agreement of the People*. Then their leaders were arrested and one of them was shot on the spot.

That was the end of the Leveller movement in England.

QUIZ FOR THE INDEPENDENTLY MINDED
(Answer on page 123.)

How many of these names were real names?

1. If-Christ-Had-Died-Thou-Hadst-Not-Been-Saved Barebone.
2. If-Christ-Had-Not-Died-Thou-Hadst-Not-Been-Saved Barebone.
3. Christ-Came-Not-Into-The-World-To-Save Barebone.
4. Praise-God Barebone.
5. If-Christ-Had-Not-Died-Thou-Hadst-Been-Saved Barebone.
6. Christ-Came-Into-The-World-To-Save-It-Not Barebone.
7. Christ-Came-Into-The-World-To-Save Barebone.
8. Praise-God-Not Barebone.
9. Praise-Barebone God.
10. If-Christ-Had-Died-Thou-Hadst-Been-Saved Barebone.

DEATH OF A KING

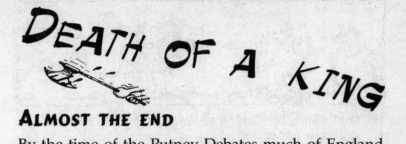

ALMOST THE END

By the time of the Putney Debates much of England was on fire with revolutionary ideas. Small wonder that Charles became worried for his safety at Hampton Court Palace, so near to London.

SCOTS PLOTS

On 11 November 1647, Charles escaped, but once again, instead of taking refuge in Europe, he chose to stay in England. He fled to Carisbrooke Castle on the Isle of Wight.

In July 1649 an army of nine thousand Scottish Presbyterians crossed the Scottish/English border to fight for Charles. What is known as the 'Second Civil War' had begun. The weather was truly dreadful and the whole lot of them were soaked to the skin as they marched south.

At that time, Scotland was seen as a dark, savage land by the English. The Civil War had spilled over into both Ireland and Scotland and in both those countries it had been far nastier than in England itself: because of hatred between Catholics and Protestants in Ireland, and because of hatred between clans in Scotland. On at least one occasion the battle cry of the Scottish Presbyterians was: 'Jesus and no quarter!'.

Cromwell led a small army north against the Scots. Always careful of his men, he stopped in the Midlands to pick up new shoes and stockings for them.

The two armies met on Preston Moor in Lancashire. By then the Scots army had grown to seventeen thousand men and Cromwell had only nine thousand - but Cromwell was a genius and the Scottish commander, the Duke of Hamilton, wasn't.

Clan is the Scottish word for a tribe. Members of a clan see themselves as belonging to the same large family.

The poor Scots were smashed.

ENOUGH IS ENOUGH!

Charles had made a big mistake by inviting the Scots to invade. As far as the Army commanders were concerned, this was an act of treason: to the English the Scots were foreigners and little better than savages. The King was taken from the Isle of Wight and brought to London under close guard.

MIND HE DOESN'T MAKE A RUN FOR IT!

Meanwhile, Henry Ireton, Cromwell's son-in-law, ordered a 'purge' of Parliament. Colonel Thomas Pride was sent to stand at the door of the House of Commons with a list of the names of around two hundred Presbyterian Members, whom he turned away. Only a 'Rump' of about 150 Independents who were friendly towards the Army were allowed in.

YOU, NOT YOU, YOU, YOU, NO NOT YOU, YOU...

1. The King escaped to the Isle of Wight (11 November 1647) - and made a secret agreement with the Scottish Presbyterians - to fight the New Model Army.

2. The New Model Army defeated the Scottish Presbyterians (Battle of Preston 17-19 August 1648).

3. The New Model Army became thoroughly disgusted with the King for inviting the Scots to fight them. They seized the King from the Isle of Wight (29 November 1648).

4. By now, thoroughly disgusted with almost everyone, the Army kicked the Presbyterians out of Parliament (*Pride's Purge*, 6 December 1648).

5. The 'Rump Parliament' (without any Presbyterians in it) tried the King for treason (20-27 January 1649).

HIS FINEST HOUR

By now Cromwell and Ireton had decided that Charles could never be trusted - he had to go. In Cromwell's terrible words:

We will cut off the King's head with the crown on it.

The Rump Parliament lost no time in setting up a court to try the King. 'Charles Stuart, the now King of England' was accused of treason. In those days a king was thought of as the father of his people, so trying the king was a bit like trying your own father. Not just England but all of Europe was shocked.

The trial took place in Westminster Hall, the large Medieval Hall which still stands beside the present Houses of Parliament. There were 135 judges, led by the President of the Court, John Bradshaw. Bradshaw's hat was lined with steel in case anyone took a pot shot at him. The hall was crammed to the rafters with members of the public.

I'LL JUST TAKE THE HAT!

Charles' trial turned out to be his finest hour. All alone, dressed in black velvet, with grey hair and looking far older than his forty-eight years, he appeared dignified and a bit sad. He refused to accept that the court had any right to try him. This, after all, was what the war had been about all along as far as he was concerned - the Divine Right of Kings to rule their subjects as they saw fit. How could subjects try their ruler when their ruler was appointed by God? Day after day Charles stood up to bullying speeches, but as he said:

... he knew not by what lawful authority he was required to make an answer.

Of course, they were going to chop his head off anyway, whatever he said or did.

And that's what they did.

THE END

On 27 January 1649, Charles was sentenced to death by 'severing of his head from his body'. Fifty-eight men signed the death warrant, including Cromwell and Ireton. (Fairfax would have nothing to do with it.) Charles was taken from the court to a room in St

James' Palace, where he said goodbye to his two youngest children, Elizabeth and Henry. The night was passed in prayer, then he was taken to the banqueting house in Whitehall Palace. Where once he had dined in state with his wife he now walked to his death. The banqueting house windows were boarded up because of the war.

They'd built a wooden scaffold outside the windows of the Banqueting House. Charles stepped on to it through the tall central window to where the block and the axeman were waiting for him, as was a large crowd held back by lines of soldiers. Charles died better than he'd lived. Even the Puritan poet Andrew Marvell was impressed:

He nothing common did or mean
Upon that memorable scene,
But with his keener eye
The axe's edge did try ...

Both the executioner and his helper were masked and wore false hair and beards in case any Royalists remembered them and took vengeance. The crowd were too far away to hear any words he might try to speak to them. After prayers and a few words to the people on the scaffold, Charles tucked his hair under his cap and lay down with his head on the block.

His head came off with a single stroke.

As the axe fell, a sort of groan went up from the large crowd. People pushed forward to dip their handkerchiefs in the royal blood. But Cromwell had taken no chances: the crowd were quickly moved away by armed cavalry.

The people walked home in shocked silence.

YOUNG KING IN OAK TREE DRAMA!

THE WHEEL TURNS FULL CIRCLE

THE KING IS DEAD, LONG LIVE THE KING!

Prince Charles was eighteen when his father was executed. He was tall, dark, charming - and clever. If he'd been king rather than his father, the tragedy would never have happened. But it did happen, and now, as far as Royalists were concerned, young Charles was the rightful King of England and Scotland. He had only one job to do, and that was to win back his crown.

In the summer of 1650 Charles II landed in Scotland from the Netherlands, and the Third Civil War began.

THE COMMONWEALTH CONQUERS

After Charles was executed, the 'Kingdom' of England had become the 'Commonwealth' of England - a Republic . It was led by Oliver Cromwell, who later became known as 'Lord Protector'. However, Scotland wasn't part of the new Commonwealth and Scotland accepted young Charles as King. On 1 January 1651, he was crowned at Scone.

Charles II led a Scottish army south into England.

The victorious army of the Commonwealth, now led by Cromwell, marched north to meet Charles' Scottish army,

Charles' army was totally defeated at the Battle of Worcester on 3 September 1651.

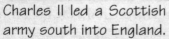 A *republic* is a country which is not ruled by a king or queen. Most modern countries are republics.

Charles escaped from Worcester and for the next six weeks he was on the run with a reward of £2,000 on his head. At one point he had to hide in an oak tree while Commonwealth soldiers searched for him below.

Finally, Charles escaped to France on a small boat, sailing from Brighthelmstone (modern Brighton).

WHERE'S THE FUN?

For the next nine years Charles II was an exile on the continent. His threadbare court moved from place to place before ending up back in the Netherlands. England had no king. The 'saints', as the Puritan sects tended to call themselves, ruled. Until he died in 1658, Cromwell, the 'Lord Protector' was their leader. The Commonwealth of saints prospered and England grew richer. Cromwell was a good leader.

But people weren't happy. The new government was Puritan - whereas the country wasn't, not really. If the truth be told, most people looked back rather fondly to the days before the war. At least then they'd been able to have some *fun*. There should be more to life than prayers and psalms.

113

Unfortunately for the 'saints' of the Commonwealth, people *like* having fun. They wanted their church ales, their wakes, their sports and dances, and their Maypoles back. They made their feelings clear in small acts of rebellion:

At Mundon in Essex the local vicar gathered a crowd on the day of a Parliament fast :

... a riotous crowd ... by drinking of healths round a joint-stool, singing of profane songs with hallooeing and roaring.

At Langford Budville twenty men who had gathered for 'cudgel play' were told to go home. But 'they came to fight and fight they would' - the authorities got a beating.

EXIT THE PROTECTOR

The Commonwealth only lasted as long as Cromwell, the strong man who ruled it. In 1657 he himself was offered the crown by members of Parliament, but he refused it because to have accepted would have made a nonsense of all he had fought for.

In August of the following year he grew sick with malaria or a 'bastard tertian ague' as his illness was

A *fast* is when people don't eat for a while. Fasts are common to most religions.

114

called at the time. Sadness at the death of his favourite daughter Elizabeth hastened his illness. He died in Whitehall Palace, where Charles I had lost his head, at 3 o'clock on the afternoon of 3 September 1658.

Cromwell had been a Puritan but no *puritan*. As well as being a great statesman he had loved music, a glass of beer or sherry and a good laugh. Such a man was bound to be missed. He was mourned by his family and by many in the country.

TUMBLEDOWN DICK DUCKS OUT

Cromwell was succeeded by his son Richard, 'Tumbledown Dick'. Dick was a decent chap but he wasn't up to the job. Republicans in the Army nudged him out of power. The Commonwealth rumbled on for another two years after Oliver's death but by then nearly everybody was fed up with it. Quite simply, it ran out of steam.

In 1660, the New Model Army marched on London. It was led by General Monck, who had decided to restore Charles II to his throne. General Fairfax came out of retirement to help him, and the original Long Parliament (those that were still alive, see page 37) was recalled. They voted to invite Charles II to return home. Meanwhile, Tumbledown Dick sailed for Paris where he lived quite happily under the name of John Clarke .

Dick returned to England in 1680 and lived out the rest of his days in Hertfordshire, still under the name of John Clarke. He died in 1712.

TIME TO PARTY

The Restoration of the monarchy with Charles II as king was one long party. To see the scenes of relief and celebration, you would hardly have guessed that they took place in the same country which had executed his father just ten years before. The diarist John Evelyn

described the scene in London when Charles arrived there on 20 May:

... the bells ringing, the streets hung with Tapissry, fountaines running with wine ... Cloth of silver, gold and vellvet every body clad in, the windos and balconies all set with Ladys ... And all this without one drop of bloud, and by that very Army, which rebell'd against him ...

And so the great English Revolution and Civil War came to an end. Charles II was not a vengeful man. Only some of the regicides, the men directly responsible for his father's execution, were executed. The bodies of Cromwell and Ireton were dug up and hung drawn and quartered. But they were dead so that didn't matter too much.

One thing is absolutely clear: Charles was no Puritan. He spelled out his ideas in his address to Parliament in 1660. He asked Parliament to join him in:

...restoring the whole Nation ... to its old good Humour and its old good Nature ... Very merry Men have been very godly Men; and if a good conscience be a continual Feast there is no Reason but Men may be very merry at it ...

As for the sectarians and the madmen, John Dryden, perhaps the greatest poet of the seventeenth century, put the argument against them in one of his many brilliant poems. His words apply equally to extremists of all religions, whether Puritan, Catholic, Jew, Muslim or Hindu. He speaks for us all - well, most of us anyway.

> *Thy God and theirs will never long agree*
> *For thine (if thou has any) must be one*
> *That lets the world and Humane-kind alone:*
> *A jolly God, that passes hours too well*
> *To promise heav'n, or threaten us with hell.*
> *That unconcern'd can at Rebellion sit;*
> *And wink at crimes he did himself commit ...*

WAS IT WORTH IT?

THE DOWN SIDE - AND THE UP SIDE

It has been calculated that 868,000 people died in the British Isles in battle and indirectly as a result of the Civil War. That's 11.6% of the population before the war, a huge price in death and suffering, even if it's peanuts by modern standards. And when it was all over, the country was back where it started - with a king on the throne. The wheel had turned full circle.

That might lead one to suppose that the whole thing was a complete waste of time, but nothing could be further from the truth. Yes, there was a king on the throne again - but there was one crucial difference to how things were before:

Charles II didn't win back the crown by an invasion - he was *invited* back.

DO YOU MIND AWFULLY IF I JUST SIGN HERE - IF YOU DON'T MIND.

And it was Parliament that did the inviting. For the next hundred odd years, while other major countries such as France were ruled by monarchs who could do pretty well whatever they liked, British kings and queens had to watch out.

If they became too unpopular, they might be sacked  . That fact had a lot to do with why Britain became the most powerful country in the world at the start of the modern era.

Rulers everywhere - take note.

That's what happened to Charles II's brother James II in the 'Glorious Revolution' of 1688.

ANSWERS TO QUIZ QUESTIONS

PAGE 9

There are one king, seven nobles, twelve gentry and eighteen common people. The dog doesn't count because it isn't a person.

PAGE 22

The cucifix and the bishop's mitre (hat). Puritans could hardly object to candles since there was no electric light in those days.

PAGE 54

The average pikeman did not carry a sketch pad, a book for light reading or a suitcase containing evening wear and swimming trunks.

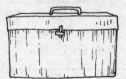

PAGE 75

1-a. That's what Thomas Tany tried to do (see page 73) - but 1-c is pretty mad behaviour too.

2-c. Abiezer Coppe used to skip and dance in front of rich men's coaches (see page 74). 2-b is pretty odd behaviour as well.

3-a. Arise Evans thought he was God (see page 74), but then 3-b is not the belief of a sane individual either.

4-a. Thomas Tany burned the Bible (see page 73). The best policy is 4-c - bannisters are expensive to replace.

Four correct answers in this section and you're clearly bonkers.

PAGE 91

Numbers two and five. Nobody, not even a Presbyterian, would speak to a king as number two is doing and number five is neither Presbyterian nor human.

PAGE 102

Numbers two, four and seven (see page 98). The rest are even more ridiculous.

INDEX

Elizabeth I 24,35
Essex, Robert Devereux, 3rd
  Earl of 86
Evans, Arise 1,74
Evelyn, John 116

Fairfax, Sir Thomas 88,101,
  108,115
festivals 17-18
Fifth Monarchists 70
Fisher, Mary 82,84
Fox, George 76,77

gentry 8,9,10,15,16,19,30,39
Glorious Revolution 121
Goring, Baron George 87
Grindletonians 70

Hamilton, Duke of 104
Hampden, John 33,41,65
Haselrig, Arthur 41
Hazard, Dorothy 80
Henrietta Maria 28-9,41,43
Henry VIII 35
Henry, Prince 25
Hervey, William 51
Hodgkins, Captain (Wicked
  Will) 58
Holles, Denzil 41
Hood, Robin 17
Hooton, Elizabeth 81
Hopkins, Mathew 85
Hopton, Sir Ralph 6

Independents 93,94,96,105
Ireton, Henry 97,105,107,
  108,118
Ironsides 66,67

James I/VI 23,24,27,28,29,
  30,35
James II 121
Jews 93
Joyce, George 96

Laud, Archbishop William
  33,34,38,39
leaguer ladies 47
Levellers 98-9,101
Lilburne, John 99
Locke, John 27
Long Parliament 37,38,115
Lunsford, Captain Thomas
  40,41

magic 84
marriage 13,78
Marston Moor, Battle of
  51,66
Marvell, Andrew 109
Mary, Queen 35
Monck, General George 115
Muggletonians 70
musketeers 47,49,50
muskets 48,50

Naseby, Battle of 87,88,89
New Model Army 67,88,93,
  94,95,96,97,98,106,115
Newbury, First Battle of 50

Parliament
  general 6,10,11,19,64,67,
    118,120
  relations with Charles I
    30-33,37,38-9,40-2,43,
    89,94,96,118,120

125

running the war 55,86
quarrels with the army
92-3,96,105-6
Peace Women 80-1
pikes 46,49,50
Presbyterians 90,93,94,103,
104,105,106
Preston, Battle of 104,106
Pride, Colonel Thomas 105
Pride's Purge 105,106
prisoners 52,53,88
Protestants 21,22,34,35,89,
104
Puritanism 19,34,35
Puritans 19,22,34,39,40,44,
53,56,66,67,68,90,113,115,
118,119
Putney Debates 98-9,101,
103
Pym, John 37,41

Quakers 71,76-7,81-3

Rainsborough, Colonel
Thomas 99
Raleigh, Sir Walter 25
Ranters 71-3,76
Roundheads 6,53,67,68,80,
86,92
Rump Parliament 105,106,
107
Rupert, Prince 55-6,62,63-
4,66
Rutland, Earl of 79

scold's bridle 78-9
Ship Money 32-3
Short Parliament 37
sieges 56-9,80

Simmonds, Martha 82
Society of Friends 76
squatters 16
Strafford, Earl of 38,39
Strode, William 41
Sultan of Turkey 82
swaddling clothes 23

Tany, Thomas 73,78
Taylor, John 43
Todd, Mary 82
toilets 14,68
trained bands 59
Trapnel, Anna 83
Turnham Green 59,61

wakes 17,114
Wellington, Duke of 52
Winstanley, Gerrard 100
Worcester, Battle of 112
Wotton, Sir Henry 63
wounds 53,84

NOW READ ON

If you want to know more about Charles I and the Civil War, see if your local library has either of these two books.

THE TRIAL AND EXECUTION OF CHARLES I
By Leonard W. Cowie (Wayland 1972). This is the story of the Civil War as told by men and women who took part in it, including Charles I and Cromwell. It's packed with fascinating pictures, many of them by eyewitnesses to the drama.

CHARGE TO VICTORY
By Annabel Brunner (Anglia Young Books 1990). The life of Oliver Cromwell in just over fifty action-packed pages, from his childhood in East Anglia to his final days as Lord Protector. This is a good, short introduction to an extraordinary man, one of the most down-to-earth geniuses who has ever lived.

ABOUT THE AUTHOR

Bob Fowke is a well-known author of children's information books. Writing under various pen names and with various friends and colleagues, he has created many unusual and entertaining works on all manner of subjects.

There's always more to his books than meets the eye - look at all the entries in the index of this one!

What They Don't Tell You About...
ORDER FORM

0 340 71330 5	ART	£3.99
0 340 63622 X	QUEEN VICTORIA	£3.99
0 340 63621 1	HENRY VIII	£3.99
0 340 69349 5	LIVING THINGS	£3.99
0 340 67093 2	SHAKESPEARE	£3.99
0 340 69350 9	STORY OF SCIENCE	£3.99
0 340 65614 X	ANCIENT EGYPTIANS	£3.99
0 340 65613 1	ELIZABETH I	£3.99
0 340 68611 1	VIKINGS	£3.99
0 340 68612 X	WORLD WAR II	£3.99
0 340 70922 7	ROMANS	£3.99
0 340 70921 9	ANGLO SAXONS	£3.99
0 340 71329 1	PLANET EARTH	£3.99
0 340 71328 3	ANCIENT GREEKS	£3.99
0 340 68995 1	STORY OF MUSIC	£3.99
0 340 73611 9	OLYMPICS	£3.99

All Hodder Children's books are available at your local bookshop or newsagent, or can be ordered direct from the publisher. Just write to the address below. Prices and availability subject to change without notice.

Hodder Children's Books, Cash Sales Department, Bookpoint, 39 Milton Park, Abingdon, Oxon, OX14 4TD, UK.
Email address: orders@bookpoint.co.uk

Please enclose a cheque or postal order made payable to Bookpoint Ltd to the value of the cover price and allow the following for postage and packing:
UK & BFPO - £1.00 for the first book, 50p for the second book, and 30p for each additional book ordered, up to a maximum charge of £3.00.
OVERSEAS & EIRE - £2.00 for the first book, £1.00 for the second book, and 50p for each additional book.

If you have a credit card you may order by telephone - (01235) 400414 (lines open 9 am - 6 pm, Monday to Saturday; 24 hour message answering service). Alternatively you can send a fax on 01235 400454.